KILLER
WHALES

Printed in Hong Kong

99   5

Library of Congress Cataloguing-in-Publication Data available upon request

ISBN 0–89658–237–X

Distributed in Canada by Raincoast Books, 112 East Third Avenue
Vancouver, B.C. V5T 1C8

Published in North America by Voyageur Press, Inc.
123 North Second Street, P.O. Box 338, Stillwater, MN 55082 U.S.A.
612–430–2210, fax 612–430–2211

Please write or call, or stop by, for our free catalog of natural history publications. Our toll-free number to place an order or to obtain a free catalog is 800–888–WOLF (9653).

Educators, fundraisers, premium and gift buyers, publicists, and marketing managers. Looking for creative products and new sales ideas? Voyageur Press books are available at special discounts when purchased in quantities, and special editions can be created to your specifications. For details contact the marketing department

Photography Copyright © 1994 by

Front Cover © Francois Gohier (Ardea)
Back Cover © Kelley Balcomb-Bartok
Page 1 © Michael Nolan (Marine Mammal Images)
Page 4 © Graeme Ellis
Page 6 © D Parer & E. Parer-Cook (Ardea)
Page 8 © Kelley Balcomb-Bartok
Page 9 © Flip Nicklin (Minden Pictures)
Page 10 © Eda Rogers (Marine Mammal Images)
Page 12 © Graeme Ellis
Page 13 © Graeme Ellis
Page 14 © Marc Webber (Planet Earth Pictures)
Page 17 © Pete Atkinson (Planet Earth Pictures)
Page 18 © Kelley Balcomb-Bartok
Page 20 © Kelley Balcomb-Bartok
Page 23 © J & S Heimlich-Boran
Page 24 © Kelley Balcomb-Bartok
Page 25 Top © J & S Heimlich-Boran
Page 25 Bottom © Kelley Balcomb-Bartok
Page 26 © Heather Angel
Page 29 © Graeme Ellis
Page 30 © Kelley Balcomb-Bartok
Page 33 © Duncan Murrell (Planet Earth Pictures)
Page 34 © Kelley Balcomb-Bartok
Page 37 © Hanne Strager
Page 38 © Jeff Foott (Bruce Colman)
Page 41 Top © Pieter Folkens (Planet Earth Pictures)

Page 41 Bottom © Kelley Balcomb-Bartok
Page 42 © D Parer & E Parer-Cook (Ardea)
Page 44 © Heather Angel
Page 46 © Duncan Murrell (Planet Earth Pictures)
Page 47 © Kelley Balcomb-Bartok
Page 49 © Pieter Folkens (Marine Mammal Images)
Page 50 © Kelley Balcomb-Bartok
Page 52 © Graeme Ellis
Page 53 © Pieter Folkens (Planet Earth Pictures)
Page 54 © Graeme Ellis
Page 55 © Francois Gohier (Ardea)
Page 56 Top Left © Ned Middleton (Planet Earth Pictures)
Page 56 Top Right © Peter Johnson (NHPA)
Page 56 Bottom Left © Heather Angel
Page 56 Bottom Right © Kelley Balcomb-Bartok
Page 57 © Flip Nicklin (Minden Pictures)
Page 58 © Jeff Foott (Bruce Colman)
Page 61 © J & S Heimlich-Boran
Page 63 © James D Watt (Planet Earth Pictures)
Page 64 © Kelley Balcomb-Bartok
Page 66 Top © Flip Nicklin (Minden Pictures)
Page 66 Bottom © Flip Nicklin (Minden Pictures)
Page 67 © Kelley Balcomb-Bartok
Page 69 © J & S Heimlich-Boran
Page 70 © Mark Carwardine (Biotica)

KILLER
WHALES

Sara & James Heimlich-Boran

Voyageur Press

Contents

Killer Whales

Long ago, in what is now south-eastern Alaska, a land rich in fish and fowl and furred creatures, Natsihlane, a skilled Tlingit Indian woodsman, went hunting with his brothers-in-law. All but the youngest were jealous of Natsihlane. They abandoned Natsihlane on a distant island, while the youngest despaired.

Natsihlane felt very sad and wondered if he would ever see his wife again. That night, a seagull came to him and flew with him to the home of the sea lions. Their chief put Natsihlane inside an inflated sea-lion stomach, laid it in the water, and instructed him to think hard about the beach near his village. He soon found himself there and began to plan revenge on his brothers-in-law.

He got different pieces of wood and began to whittle blackfish. He tried spruce, then red cedar, then hemlock, painting each in stripes of different colours. But no amount of singing or shouting would bring them alive.

Finally, he carefully carved fine yellow cedar into eight large and small blackfish. He painted each with a white band across the head and a white circle on the dorsal fin. He sang his most powerful songs for them, commanding them to go. They swam about, and soon the bay was full of spray from their spouting and playing.

After many days, Natsihlane saw his brothers-in-laws' canoe far out at sea. He commanded the blackfish to destroy all but the youngest. They swam out and around and around the canoe. The men and the craft disappeared, but two blackfish saved the youngest brother-in-law and carried him towards the shore.

Natsihlane called the blackfish to him and said: 'When I made you I did not intend that you should kill human beings. I made you to get revenge on my brothers-in-law. Hereafter you shall not harm human beings but help them when they are in trouble. Now go.' And they swam out to sea, the first killer whales in the world.

Adapted from a Tlingit Indian folktale

Killer whales, the most dramatic and the largest of the dolphins, feature in legends from all parts of the globe. The mythological powers attributed to them and many other large mammals reflect the active human imagination, sparked by the impressive qualities of the living animals.

As researchers who have had 17 years of privileged familiarity with a group of killer whales, we recall our first impressions vividly: a white eye patch and grey dorsal saddle the only visible clues of a large being in the depths of velvety-green waters; a dark body discernible only just before breaking the surface with a blow; the swoop of a back and the immensity of a dorsal fin; the grace of a roll through the water; the flip of a wide tail at the end of a breathing sequence; the sweep of exhaled breath drifting across your face; a white belly and black back suspended against a blue sky during an exuberant, high, backwards jump.

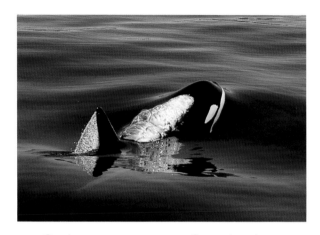

Orcinus orca *emerges from the deep.*

Each time we see killer whales, we are reminded how strange and remarkable it is that these creatures, which move with such ease through the three-dimensional and highly dynamic marine world, are mammals like us; that while we share much of the same basic anatomy and both breathe air, they are supremely adapted to a watery environment which would, without artificial support, kill us terrestrial mammals.

Known by early whalers as 'whale killers', killer whales once had a reputation as voracious predators killing on a whim; stories of their attacks on boats and people fuelled the aura of menace. Concentrated efforts to understand them began only after the first killer whale capture in the early 1960s. Since then, as details of their lives in captivity and in the wild have been revealed, many long-held misconceptions about killer whales, harboured over centuries, have been replaced with evidence of an astoundingly complex creature. Reflecting changing attitudes, the common name for the species is becoming 'orca', which derives from the scientific name, *Orcinus orca*.

*Exuberant leaps are common and add to the
drama which has inspired generations of
story-tellers, poets, and artists.*

Looking into the eye of a killer whale,
an oceanic mammal.

Most of our knowledge of killer whales comes from long-term studies in Washington State and British Columbia – the North American Pacific Northwest. The first observations, begun in 1971 by scientists of the Canadian Pacific Biological Station, were planned to provide a population estimate for killer whales in Canada. Capture operations had been ongoing since the mid-1960s. In order to decide whether they should be continued, the Canadian government wanted to know how many killer whales were left.

After an initial summer-long survey along north-eastern Vancouver Island, the researchers returned the following year and recognised some of the same individual killer whales by distinctive scars and marks on their dorsal fins and backs. They decided to create a photographic catalogue of individuals as a tool for counting the population. A careful examination and comparison of photographs, collected in hundreds of hours of observation at sea, provided a count of killer whales frequenting the inland waters off eastern Vancouver Island.

The most exciting discovery in those early days was that these killer whales lived in three different groups, which never interacted with one another. The group regularly found off north-eastern Vancouver Island was named the northern resident community. At the end of 1976, when the research conclusions were reported, it totalled 123 whales. A smaller group consistently ranged off south-eastern Vancouver Island and was called the southern resident community. These two communities never crossed the central region of Vancouver Island into each others' territories. However, a group of around 75 killer whales sporadically roamed throughout both precincts, and were referred to as the transient community.

Alarmingly, the researchers discovered that nearly all live captures for display in aquariums had been of whales from the southern resident community. Forty-eight whales had been removed from the southern resident population in the 1960s and 1970s, and only 80 remained by 1976. It was clear that captures could no longer be allowed from this community.

Our own work with killer whales began in 1976 when the government of the United States decided to conduct a study to compare the Canadian research results with killer whale observations from adjacent US waters. A host of researchers have come and gone since those first efforts, keeping a diversity of studies alive, monitoring the population growth in the region, and contributing to our understanding of how killer whales live. Other research sites have sprung up in locations as diverse as Norway and Argentina, with preliminary findings very similar to the US and Canadian results.

We now recognise that killer whales have specialised feeding strategies, developed to exploit the prominent food resource at hand. We have discovered that groups of killer whales, including residents and transients, are not only different in feeding strategy, group size, and social structures, but are actually distinct genetic races. And, especially in the case of residents and transients, to find such striking differences between two groups of the same species exploiting the same habitat is unusual.

Tail flukes are adaptations to a water habitat.

We now accept that killer whales have a long lifespan, equivalent to that of humans, and live in highly social, co-operative groups, organised through complex vocal repertoires distinct to each group. In captivity, they have surprised us with their ability to learn dialects from other whales and have proved to be inquisitive, often gentle, and easily trained.

Whether free or captive, killer whales continue to evoke the interest of scientists and public alike. Since the mid 1970s, the attention they have received has increased dramatically. Each investigation, whether experimental or observational enriches our understanding of these unique marine mammals.

A family cluster completely at ease in their marine world.

Oceanic Mammals

We had been following killer whales through the lustrous afternoon: a lazy meandering while they fished, with long pauses for deep dives. Everything was still and relaxed. Without warning, Merlin, a large male, rose vertically through the surface, almost rubbing against the boat. First the blunt snout, then the rounded black head, scattering diamond-bright water droplets, then the white patch above the eye, and then the eye itself, brown and intent. In that instant, we realised how truly well-adapted whales and dolphins are for their marine environment. While we clung to the boat, dependent on it for our survival in an environment alien to our land-adapted anatomy, the killer whale moved easily and with confidence. Yet we were both warm-blooded, milk-producing, air-breathing mammals, looking eye-to-eye. And, like us, killer whales have risen to the top of the food chain, able to survive in a variety of habitats.

Personal Diary, August

'Bufeo de mascarilla', 'Spaekhuggare', 'Sadshi', 'Mesungesak', 'Kosatka', 'Innuatu': local names for killer whales in Spain, Sweden, Japan, Alaska, Russia, and Korea, and just a few of the hundreds found around the world, reflect the mammals' ability to live in every ocean and to thrive in a wide range of habitats. From prehistoric rock paintings to modern ship-based censuses, killer whales have been reported from nearly every corner of the globe. Although killer whales are most common over the continental shelf in cooler seas near the North and South Poles, very little is known of their movements on a global scale and there is no reliable estimate of the world population.

Clusters of killer whales were commonly encountered by whalers across the entire North Atlantic. Although no longer common in some of the areas they once inhabited, killer whales still roam the coasts of North Africa and continental Europe and, infrequently, into the Mediterranean. They are regular visitors to British and Irish waters between April and September, particularly along the Atlantic seaboard, the Western Isles and in the North Sea. As in Norwegian and Icelandic waters, they are probably following the movements of spawning Atlantic salmon and herring.

In the eastern Pacific, Pre-Christian peoples from the Chukchi Sea to the equator commonly encountered killer whales. The Nasca of Peru worshipped killer whales and built temples dedicated to them. Killer whales are now most commonly found along the coasts of the Alaskan Peninsula, Prince William Sound in the Gulf of Alaska, Georges Strait and around Vancouver Island in British Columbia, and Puget Sound, Washington State; this Northwest Coast population is considered one of the world's most dense. They also occur off the coasts of Oregon, California, Baja California and the Gulf of California, Mexico, and between Cabo San Lucas and the Galapagos Islands off South America. Although there is a concentration off Japan, there is little evidence that killer whales were ever common in the mid-oceanic Pacific.

One of the best indications of the current distribution of killer whale concentrations is the location where field studies are being conducted. In addition to the Pacific Northwest, there are projects in southern Alaska, Argentina, Norway, Iceland, and Marion Island and the Crozet Islands in the Indian Ocean. According to the latest available censuses, 335 individuals have been identified in the Pacific Northwest, 232 in Prince William Sound, Alaska, 26 in Argentina, around 350 in Norway, 143 in Iceland and 76 in the Crozet Islands. Appearance, behaviour, and some biological traits differ in each of these populations, indicating long-term adjustments to the local environment.

These populations may have originated from larger aggregations ranging the wider ocean basins. Killer whales observed at sea are reported in groups of two to three hundred, yet remain subdivided into smaller clusters spaced from several hundred yards to a half mile apart. Although it has been suggested that there is one population in the Pacific, cruising a territory which covers the vast expanse of ocean between Asia and America and between the two poles, it is more plausible that there are clumped populations which roam through specific ranges, their movements governed by seasonal changes in the environment and prey.

The coastal pockets with localised killer whales populations typically possess abundant marine life, especially fish. The passage of many generations is required for killer whale communities to become established in such coastal areas: a slow behavioural and social adaptation to abundant local resources, reflecting long-standing forces affecting killer whale evolution.

Saddle patch pattern and dorsal fin shape are unique to each individual killer whale, just as hair colour and face shape are unique to every human.

The ancestors of all whales and dolphins were extinct land mammals, which also gave rise to modern cows, horses, sheep and other ungulates. Millions of years ago, they lived at the edge of a great inland sea, long before the earth's continents shifted into the positions they now hold. Over time and for unknown reasons, their descendants gradually moved into the sea, their bodies adapting for survival in an alien environment. Primitive whales first appeared around 50–60 million years ago. Most of the modern types had appeared by 20 million years ago.

Class, Order, Family, Genus, Species. These are the five basic levels which make up a scientific address for all organisms on Earth. Like a postal address, organised in order of country, area or postal code, city, street and number, each level in the hierarchy serves to clarify the exact position of an organism in the general scheme of life. In this classification system, each division is based on commonly held characteristics, beginning with the most general and ending with the most specific. The basic two-part scientific name for each organism combines its genus and species names and reflects its place and connections to other organisms. Killer whales are scientifically known as *Orcinus orca*: their genus name meaning 'belonging to the realms of the dead' and their species name a derivative of Orcus, an ogre and Roman god of the underworld. Whales and dolphins belong to the Class *Mammalia*, Order *Cetacea*. They are collectively known as cetaceans and are divided into two suborders: those with teeth, called the *Odontoceti*, and those with baleen, called the *Mysticeti*.

The *Odontoceti* are subdivided into families by tooth type, skull structure and other anatomical characteristics. The *Delphinidae* are just one of several toothed cetacean families and embrace all dolphins. Killer whales, *Orcinus orca*, are anatomically similar to smaller dolphins and have been placed in this family. Yet their larger size, round head, blunt 'beak', and fewer teeth are characteristics shared with other globe-headed species, like pilot whales. This has caused debate about their classification, with some taxonomists arguing they should belong to a group called the *Globicephalinae*.

The *Delphinidae* originated around 11 million years ago. Killer whales are one of the oldest delphinid types and branched off very early from the main evolutionary group. Through time, delphinids underwent refinements on the basic type, each genera developing specialised adaptations. Killer whales, compared to

The killer whale tuxedo comes in only one model world-wide
and does not change during an individual life.

other delphinids, have fewer modifications to the general plan and principally specialised a large body size to exploit large prey.

There appears to be more than one type, or race, of killer whale. Along with variations in pigmentation, size and some behaviours, genetic differences have been detected. Differences at this level are, in geological terms, comparatively recent and correspond to the end of the last ice age. The residents and transients living in the Pacific Northwest are genetically distinct and probably began to evolve separately around two million years ago. Genetic differences also occur between the two resident groups and probably began to emerge 40,000 years ago, when killer whales colonised the area. Separated by a tidal boundary which provides a natural barrier, the two communities have had little contact and remain genetically isolated.

Killer whales cannot be confused with any other species, anywhere in the world. Their large size, robust shape, tall dorsal fins, oval flippers and striking coloration are very characteristic and immediately recognisable. Females generally attain a length of 7.0 m (7.66 yds) and can weigh up to 3,100 kg (6,835.5 lbs). Males grow longer, up to 8.2 m (8.98 yds) and 4,000 kg (8,820 lbs). Calves are born measuring about 2.2 m (2.4 yds) long and weighing around 180 kg (397 lbs).

Killer whales have proportionately higher dorsal fins than other dolphins, from one-tenth to one-fifth of the total body length. The dorsal fins of males can grow up to 1.8 m (1.97 yds) in height and stand more than twice as high as those of adult females. The height of the dorsal fin is a useful way to distinguish adult males, but as it doesn't begin to grow until around age 10 and takes at least another seven years to reach its full height, distinguishing between subadult males and adult females is difficult.

The uniquely-shaped, paddle-like pectoral flippers are also proportionately larger than other dolphins' and contrast with the sickle-shaped flippers of most delphinids. They lie about one-fourth of the distance from the snout to the flukes. In males, flippers may reach 2 m (2.19 yds); about 20% of the body length; the flippers in females reach 11–13%.

Many dolphins and porpoises have complex pigmentation patterns, yet killer whales wear a tidy black and white tuxedo affair. This simple counter-shading is believed to be the most generalised and probably also the most primitive within the dolphin family.

The white shirt-front extends from the lower jaw down to the genital region, with the dark coat wrapping around the flippers to lie slightly open over the belly, revealing the genital area in a tri-section cut-away which closes smartly at the base of the tail. The cut of the dark coat is not quite identical in both sexes and the shape of the white genital field reveals the sex of the individual. Males generally have a long, narrow middle section, while females sport a wide, almost circular shape. The faces of the flukes are also light-coloured, as are the jaunty eye patches resting behind and above each eye. Wrapped just behind the dorsal fin is a grey patch in the shape of a horse saddle.

The basic pattern of a killer whale's suit at birth will remain fundamentally unchanged throughout its life. Very young calves are occasionally mistaken for porpoises: the saddle patch is often quite dark and the light-pigmented areas are commonly butterscotch or rusty-hued. But, before the end of the first year, the saddle dims to grey and the colours fade to white.

Variations in the pattern of the saddle are unique to individual killer whales. Researchers working on wild, free-ranging populations can recognise most individuals by the saddle's shape and pattern and confirm their notes with photographs of the individuals they observe. Photographic identification is the fundamental tool for following an individual in its daily activities, throughout its life.

Each population bears slight variations to the general design. Killer whales off Australia and New Zealand have been described as dark purplish-brown with ivory-hued areas. Killer whales in the Antarctic are smaller and distinctly more yellow than their northern relatives, and those off Mexico and in the southern hemisphere have plain, featureless saddle patches, as do the transients of British Columbia and Washington State. Resident killer whales have complex saddle patch features, and are significantly different from transients in the area.

Such variations in appearance come about from long-term isolation of killer whale communities. Killer whales are first isolated geographically, then reproductively, then genetically. Variations also eventually occur in the social fabric and account for the differences in the societies of residents and transients.

These Pacific Northwest killer whales are genetically different to their Argentinean cousins, but look similar.

The towering dorsal fin takes several years to develop and indicates a fully-adult male.

Very young calves lose their pink hues and grow
rapidly within the first six months

Family Ties

We were happy to see the end of the bad weather and get back onto the water. For weeks, we had been land-bound by black, storm-filled clouds and wild grey seas, watching from shore as the killer whales ploughed through the churning waters, oblivious to the screaming winds and nasty winter chill. We had been in the boat only a few minutes when young whales Blossom and Slick arrived, dallying in the calmer waters of the bay. Both were approaching maturity that year. Blossom had filled out and finally looked more like an adult female. We wondered if she would soon show up with her own calf. Slick's dorsal fin was slightly more elongated, but he still looked young. We knew it would be several more years before he gained the tall adult-male fin. We were fond of these older adolescents and could only hope they would live their maximum life span. On that fine day, watching them meander in the kelp beds, we knew Blossom could look forward to a very long life, but Slick's would be much shorter.

Personal Diary, February

Killer whales can lead very long lives and they have a complex life history. An astonishing story has unfolded through the long years of research on wild groups in the Pacific Northwest. At first some of the details seemed unbelievable. Yet, after 20 years of concentrated research, it is confirmed that killer whales exhibit some of the rarest traits in the mammalian plan. Humans are one of the few similar mammalian types.

As with humans, female killer whales live longer than males, up to 80 years, while males generally manage only 50–60 years. There is no single reason for this. Being a large male with all that body mass to feed and push through the water could simply be too stressful for a long life. Males certainly have greater food requirements to maintain their greater body size. They may also have a more stressful role in group protection. Perhaps even competition for access to females is more dangerous than has been observed. The road to sexual, physical, and social maturity is a slow one, very much like our own. Until the age of about 10 years, there is little difference in how males and females develop.

Male killer whales reach sexual maturity at around age 15, in the midst of their adolescent growth. This is the time when the male dorsal fin begins to grow noticeably taller and when he starts to produce sperm. It does not mean, however, that he is socially ready, or permitted, to father calves. Social maturity occurs much later, when a male has become a fully-grown adult and can pursue mates. In humans, the period between sexual maturity and social maturity is the transition period from childhood to adulthood, when the rules of adult society are learned. The long period in killer whales is parallel. It is common in many mammals, exemplified by roving bands of 'bachelor' males, very similar to human teenagers.

Female killer whales mature sexually between 12 and 16 years of age and stop growing by the age of 18. Females in captivity ovulate throughout the year and exhibit 'spontaneous ovulation', meaning that they continue to ovulate even without the presence of a male. This is not common in mammals.

Calves take between 15 and 17 months to develop in the womb. So, theoretically, an adult female could give birth as frequently as every two years. But calves nurse for most of their first two years and this can influence the mother's next pregnancy. Weaning usually takes place towards the end of the second year, but can be prolonged if no other sibling appears.

An adult female is capable of producing around five calves over a 25 year period. Yet not all adult females produce calves like clockwork. The shortest observed gap between births is 2 years and the longest 12 years. If a calf dies at birth (and as many as 40% do so), a female may give birth again much sooner than normal.

Female killer whales appear to stop bearing calves in later life, rather like human females; an extremely uncommon trait in mammals. As most female mammals age, they decline in reproductive output but do not stop reproducing completely. However, many female killer whales in the Pacific Northwest have not had new calves for many years. Those who remain without a new calf for longer

*This family group of Canadian killer whales is part of a
multi-generational pod which consists of several other family groups. Each
group or subpod generally travels separately from the rest of the pod. The
female pictured to the right is accompanied by her two uncles.*

Females and their offspring remain together throughout their lives.

than 10 years are defined as 'post-reproductive'; living beyond their child-bearing years. Using a variety of age estimates, it appears that half of all killer whale females older than 39 have stopped giving birth and by the age of 55, all females are post-reproductive. Although there is no direct proof that ovulation has ceased, biological studies on short-finned pilot whales, a closely related species, have shown a lack of ovulation in females over the age of 40. This strongly supports the existence of this later life stage in female killer whales. It has been estimated that one-third of all adult females in the Pacific Northwest resident communities are post-reproductive.

These females may live 20 or more years after giving birth for the last time. The 20 to 30 year difference in male and female lifespans means the oldest members of any pod are most likely to be females. Mothers and even grandmothers will therefore often be alive throughout their sons' entire lives, but not their daughters'.

These life history parameters deeply affect the nature of killer whale society. Long periods of development and maturation provide increased exposure to the behaviours of elders and allows for the inter-generational transfer of skills. The longer life-spans of the females gives them greater experience and makes them the crucial element in the social structure.

The bulk of our knowledge about the social structure of killer whale groups is based on studies of resident communities in British Columbia and Washington State. The infrequent occurrence of transient killer whale groups has kept our knowledge about their social structure and group dynamics extremely limited. The story we can tell is based on one type of killer whale, living in a very specific habitat and exploiting a very specific food source. Killer whales living in other locations experience different pressures working on them and may have developed slightly different strategies.

Mother-calf pairs are the core of killer whale society and the structure of groups follows maternal lines. Bonds between adult females and offspring of both sexes are long-term and last well into adulthood, creating basic units of an adult female and her offspring, including adult sons. Typically, the unit will contain an older post-reproductive female, a mother with up to four calves of varying ages, and an adult male.

A 'pod' is made up of several such maternal sub-groups which are closely related. A rarity in mammals, neither males nor females leave the pod, but remain in the group into which they were born for their entire lifetime. Killer whale pods seem to be extended families of mothers, sisters, brothers, aunts, uncles, nieces, nephews, and cousins. But there do not appear to be any fathers.

Since the males and females are closely related, it is unlikely that any breeding takes place within the pod. Why? When sex between killer whales has been witnessed it has been between males and females from different pods. Calves are more likely products of matings between pods, rather than in pods. This avoids inbreeding and means pods are stable, non-breeding kin groups.

A community is simply several pods which live in the same area and frequently travel together. These larger communities are the breeding unit of associated pods. Genetic testing could tell us about the relatedness of individuals in a pod and in the larger community. Until such tests are carried out, we are left to combine speculation, observations from the field and theories of social biology to determine how this unique system could have developed.

Like most species of dolphins, killer whales are sexually promiscuous. Adult females are not only sexually active all year round, but also ovulate throughout the year. This means adult males have no guarantee which offspring might be theirs.

Having offspring, and investing time to guarantee their survival, is nature's way of passing genes on through time, and all creatures follow some sort of strategy for future representation of their genes. But, if a female killer whale is mating with many males, who is to know which male fathered which calf?

Other male mammals herd females into harems, corralling them in jealously-guarded territories and controlling access. Killer whales, living in the three-dimensional, boundary-less oceanic environment, have no such control.

A male killer whale can deal with this problem by mating with as many females as possible. This would flood the market, increasing his chances of producing offspring and having his genes represented in the next generation. But, since he cannot be guaranteed paternity, it is not cost

Alaskan killer whales cluster around adult females,
the matriarchs of killer whale societies.

Close social bonds unite killer whale society.

effective for him to contribute paternal care to the offspring of any females he mates with. It is not in his best interests to invest time in calves which may be the offspring of other males.

Under these circumstances, an adult male is better off caring for the offspring of his sisters or his younger siblings, which he knows are kin. Although these calves are not passing on genes descending directly from him, they are carrying genes he has in common with his mother or sisters. Part of his genetic structure is guaranteed to go on. This is how an adult male killer whale can improve upon his 'reproductive success'.

Critical to the social bond holding pods and communities together are the older adult females who have passed their calf-bearing years. Alternatively called 'grannies', 'aunties', or 'allo-mothers', they have no dependent calves of their own but spend time, almost exclusively, with the calves of particular mothers. Looked at as game strategy, this has several important benefits.

If a female had calves up until her death, she would leave motherless calves to fend for themselves, cutting down their chances of survival. But a female who stops having calves at a certain age is able to successfully raise her last calf to maturity and ensure her own genes are passed onto another generation. If she then also takes over some of the parenting of her grand-calves as they grow older, she helps her daughter to produce the most calves possible. If an adult female loses her own calves but helps to raise those of her closest kin, she will achieve a modicum of success. Like the adult males, she will be making an investment in the larger gene pool which she shares with her sisters.

As the oldest members of any pod are usually females, they will have greater experience in dealing with the problems of survival. The oceanic environment is very complex. There is a great deal of ocean craft to learn: where to find food and how to catch it; how to travel and stay oriented in a three-dimensional world; which routes are best and what obstacles to avoid; how to deal with shifting currents, temperatures, and depths; how to recognise kin and community and learn the social rules that exist. The longevity and survival skills of the older females increase their importance to the society.

The complex detail of killer whale societies is paralleled only by the societies of elephants and higher primates, again including humans. Although we cannot be certain of its accuracy, we can paint a picture of how a killer whale fits into its society through its lifetime.

As a young calf, a killer whale is accepted as part of the social fabric of the pod through its relationship with its mother. It will have open access to all members of the pod, playing with other calves, darting amongst the adolescents, wrestling with the older males. All pod members will participate in its care, even adult males. In the Pacific Northwest, Norway and Argentina, males of all ages engage in baby-sitting and educational duties.

During adolescence, relationships with killer whales of its own age develop while most others grow weak. Family alliance is dependent on keeping a close relationship with a 'granny'. With full adulthood, dependency upon these 'allo-mothers' declines and direct affiliations with mothers are re-established.

Females have a more integrated place in the society than males, as a result of the dependency on their female kin as they enter the reproductive pool and receive aid in raising offspring. Apart from close affiliations with their mothers, adult males tend to form alliances amongst themselves. With age, mothers become reproductively inactive and take over support roles.

Distinct sub-groups form through the interplay of a female's age and the number, ages and sex of her offspring. Two scenarios are possible, though in both, adult sons stay with their mothers. An older female with several offspring may stay with her youngest daughter (and her offspring), continuing to function as an 'allo-mother', while her older and more experienced adult daughters (and their offspring) disengage from the larger maternal group and form separate subgroups. However, an older female having only one or two adult daughters may stay closely associated with both, maintaining direct contact throughout her lifetime.

New lineages or pods may form as the older females die out, or as the degree of relatedness between kin begins to thin. Given the long lifespan of killer whales, the formation of new pods is likely to take many decades.

The Daily Regime

Blossom lay on her back, whacking her flukes on the water. Slick was still meandering in the kelp bed, letting the long leaves slip along his head, over his dorsal fin and down his back with what seemed erotic delight. In the distance, the rest of their pod was travelling leisurely, lined up abreast of one another. From the charts on our boat, we could see they were swimming over fairly featureless terrain. As they approached the small rise where the 50 foot long bull kelp grew, they slowed and began to mill around. We waited while they took a short break, little calves pushing floating feathers around on their snouts, adults resting at the surface, making soft farting noises from their blow-holes. Up ahead was a narrow channel where the tide rushed through as it changed through its cycles. Soon, the pod moved on. As expected, they began to porpoise through the swirls and eddies, breaching out of the water and becoming thoroughly boisterous, as if they enjoyed the rough playground. We were beginning to be able to predict not only the sequence of their changing behaviours, but what sort of place they would do certain things in.

Personal Diary, June

As long-term studies unfold, we are becoming aware that differences in location affect how populations of killer whales cope with their environment. Every year, new forms of basic behaviours are revealed, showing us how adaptable killer whales can be. Patterns of behaviour probably represent cultural mechanisms which have been learned through trial and error and passed down through the generations. If studies in non-American/Canadian waters continue to receive support, they will undoubtedly uncover new variations. Until the results of more studies are available, our picture is simply another summary of killer whales living in British Columbia and Washington State.

Killer whales in the two resident communities organise what they do into a fairly predictable pattern. They travel, searching for schools of fish as they go, and when conditions are right, they begin feeding. After an active hunt and good meal, they settle down for a rest. Upon waking, they break into a round of boisterous socialising before recommencing their travels.

Southern killer whales spend just under half their time foraging, a quarter of it travelling, and resting and socialising about equally the rest of the time. Northern killer whales do things a bit differently: over half of their time is taken up in foraging, and only a small proportion in travelling, but almost a quarter of their time is spent on resting and socialising. Transient killer whales are different again: foraging takes up the bulk of their time, travelling just over an eighth, and play only a tiny fraction. They have yet to be seen resting.

Whether in single groups or multi-pod gangs, travelling killer whales always move at a good pace in a rather determined style, going from place to place in ranked formations. Moving from one feeding area to another, they usually travel across deep, featureless areas. Although they have been observed travelling for up to 5.5 hours at one stretch, an average trip lasts around an hour.

Cetaceans do not sleep as other mammals do. It is more like an alert restfulness. Resting killer whales move extremely slowly and methodically in tight clusters, often touching one another, breathing synchronously in shallow rising and falling waves, always silent. Sometimes one or two on the periphery may be on watch, herding other pod members away from obstacles. Resting in stretches of around two hours, killer whales usually choose protected areas away from the main tidal flow. Needing to swim all the time (they would otherwise sink), they occasionally face into a current, using it to stay in one place instead of moving forward.

Socialising killer whales undertake a wide variety of physical activities and aerial displays, usually in open water areas with underlying kelp-covered sills which generate strong upwelling currents. Playing with inanimate objects, breaching contests (where adults and calves alike come bursting out of the water), belly flops, slapping, rolling and thrashing at the surface, and spyhops (vertical rises on the surface to take in a view from above), are all characteristic play activities. Socialising in multi-pod groups commonly includes sexual interactions. Penile erections in adult and sub-adult males seem to take on an advertising quality as they are waved around in the air.

Activities, like fluke-waving and playing with inanimate objects, may help to keep hunting skills fine-tuned.

Catching seals on sharply-pitched beaches in Argentina is a learned technique, requiring patience and skill.

Greeting ceremonies are unique to southern killer whales. When reunited after a separation of a day or more, each pod forms a row, and hovers at the surface facing the other pod. They then swarm into each other, each individual rubbing and rolling against the others. This also happens when pods awaken after a multi-pod resting session and, like social ceremonies in wild dogs and elephants, appears to re-affirm social bonds.

Beach rubbing is unique to northern whales and constitutes 4.5% of their activity. Pods frequently interrupt foraging sessions with visits to a specific 0.5 km section of shoreline on Vancouver Island to rub themselves against two small pebble shelves 3 to 6 m deep. They dive to the bottom and rub for up to a minute at a time. Bouts last up to 1.5 hours and are often accompanied by resting and socialising.

When foraging and feeding, resident killer whales work in multi-pod groups, usually scattered over a large area in a mixture of small subgroups and individuals and travelling erratically. High-speed swimming with sudden changes in direction, surface lunges and long dive times, and the occasional percussive splash indicate active pursuit or herding of fish. Whereas residents feed in areas of high relief sub-surface topography and along salmon migratory routes, transients feed in shallow protected areas around concentrations of marine mammals.

More than any other behaviour, the two entirely different foraging strategies of resident and transient killer whales reflect the essential differences between them.

Killer whales are supremely efficient predators. Some might think them tame and playful in captivity, and the name killer whale an unfair one. But in the wild, killer whales do kill, with distinct division of labour and a minimum of fuss. Their reputation as indiscriminate killers has come from a variety of often misinterpreted observations. Famous for preying on other marine mammals, including the largest baleen whales, killer whales actually feed on a diversity of other species: birds, fish, squid, octopus, even sea turtles. But they are not generalised and opportunistic feeders. They specialise on prey abundant in their particular area, while having the flexibility to shift their preferences in response to changes in prey abundance.

Like top predators on the African savannah, killer whales live alongside prey species in bouts of neutral coexistence. They mix with pilot whales in the Faroe Islands, and travel with sperm whales and

Risso's dolphins off South Africa. Killer whales and minke whales sometimes feed together in Puget Sound: the minke whales and salmon feeding on small fish fry at the surface and the killer whales hunting the salmon.

Killer whales prey on all marine mammal families, except for river dolphins and manatees. Their seemingly blood-thirsty habits are actually efficient foraging strategies. Young or weak marine mammals are preferred, although killer whales can co-operate to kill healthy adult baleen whales. Most hunts of large whales seem to require groups of more than five killer whales, but success is possible in smaller groups. Sperm whales are rarely killed, and only attacked when with calves.

Seals are hunted by single killer whales and by gangs acting co-operatively. Seal tossing is an effective killing method. Killer whales have been observed regurgitating seal pelts: hitting them out of the water may loosen meat from skin, even tenderising it.

In Argentina, adult males intentionally strand themselves on steep gravel beaches where they can capture seals and sea lions. Without killing them, the adult killer whales tow them offshore, release them and stand by as younger killer whales move in for the recapture, practising behaviour they will need as adults. The prey is probably disabled or disoriented and is easy to catch, especially away from the shelter of land. Such 'food sharing' has also been observed between adult males; probably because they were closely related and food supply was limited.

Off the Crozet Islands in the Indian Ocean, where the slope up the beach is more shallow than in Argentina, it is predominantly adult females that use the stranding technique of hunting. Here, young killer whales imitate the intentional stranding behaviour of their mothers. Calves practise with another female if their mother is not accomplished at stranding.

Surplus killing occurs infrequently. It may happen for teaching, play, or plain aggression. More commonly, killer whales will consume selected parts of some prey, optimising the most energy-rich tidbits.

Fish are as important in the killer whale diet as mammals. Thirty-one species of fish have so far been recorded as killer whale prey. Even where marine mammal predation is common, fish still make up a portion of killer whale stomach contents.

*An Alaskan killer whale takes a shallow
dive into a group of fish herded against
the shoreline.*

Killer whales use co-operative hunting techniques for fish as well; the degree of co-operation being dependent on the fish's behaviour. If the fish live in very tightly grouped schools, co-operative hunting may be more beneficial than if the fish travel solitarily or in loose, small schools.

In Norway, killer whales enter the fjords when groups of herring, a very tightly schooling fish, concentrate for spawning. When they locate a school they begin circling around it, turning sideways and flashing their white bellies to scare the fish and keep them concentrated. This requires a fair degree of organisation and co-operation. They must avoid collisions while remaining close enough to keep the herring from escaping, and must also show some degree of restraint: if they all fed at once, the 'carousel' would stop and the fish escape. The killer whales also take turns slapping their massive tail flukes through the school, creating a loud, explosive noise, like the cracking of a whip. Any fish in the path of this tail are stunned or killed and can be picked off at leisure.

The red gills of salmon are sometimes discarded.

In the Pacific Northwest, salmon, a moderately schooling fish, is the abundant food source. Killer whales show some degree of co-operation in herding them into concentrations, travelling in a broad, line-abreast flank, splashing with their flukes and flippers, making noise which drives the fish ahead of them. They bunch the salmon against underwater barriers, such as shorelines and seamounts. Once the fish are concentrated, the killer whales feed individually.

Although co-operation is needed in feeding on both marine mammals and fish, the two prey types require different and very specific hunting techniques. The difference in behavioural skills is sufficient to affect the size and structure of killer whale groups, as well as breeding behaviour. This specialisation in the exploitation of different food sources has led to the existence of the two different kinds of killer whales: residents and transients.

During the early years of research, scientists noticed that transients occurred in smaller groups and produced far fewer calves. They were thought to be 'less successful' than resident killer whales. And, because they wandered along the jagged coastline and dead-end bays, they appeared lost in unfamiliar territory.

Now it is clear that the two types are simply specialists. The smaller groups of the transients are the optimal size for capturing marine mammal prey. Their lower reproductive rates may even be related to the numbers of marine mammals available, which are lower compared to the numbers of fish available. It is also clear that the wandering of transients into odd corners is simply their method of exploiting the habitat of seals; while the residents are doing the same by staying in the main channels where the salmon run.

There is an interwoven ecological web between the residents and transients in the Pacific Northwest, which establishes an equilibrium between them. Salmon and seals feed on small fish. Seals also feed on salmon and compete with resident killer whales. Transient killer whales prefer seals. As residents eat more salmon there is less available for the seals, which decrease in number and provide less food for transients. However, fewer salmon allows the numbers of small fish to increase, which provides more food for the seals and eventually more food for the transients.

These complex interactions suggest resident and transient killer whales actually benefit from exploiting the same habitat, and thus their groups may be larger than either type would be on its own.

Predators throughout the world often specialise on whatever prey is available, but for members of the same species occurring in the same habitat, to exploit different food niches, and to have genetic differences, is very rare.

Killer whales may have lost their reputation
as rapacious, frenzied killers, but this Dall's porpoise
knows all too well the efficiency of killer
whale predators.

Sound as a Tool

We couldn't see killer whales, but we could hear them through the underwater microphone. Their squeaks, groans and whistles were mild, so we knew they had to be at least five miles away. The sounds became louder as they headed our way. Suddenly, there was a deafening singsong *Bree-fftt-whirreep* and a cluster of echolocation clicks, making the needle on the tape recorder jump off the scale. Somebody had snuck up and investigated the hydrophone. Slick, in the middle of a group of playful, boisterous killer whales, swept by us in a wave of noise: Bronx squawks blasting out of their blowholes at the surface and wolf-whistles screeching underwater. As they moved off, we ran out of tape and hauled up the hydrophone in frustration. But we could still hear their surface calls, 500 feet away.

Personal Diary, September

In the marine environment, where light, space and distances take on aspects almost unfathomable to terrestrial animals, sound is a most efficient survival tool. All dolphins use streams of echolocation clicks for navigation and locating food and more elaborate calls for communication. The killer whale's intricate social fabric and co-ordinated movement is maintained through acoustic communication.

The vocal tradition of resident killer whale pods is complex and conveys a wide variety of information, from the location of an individual to the activity and general emotional state of the pod. Communication calls are made up of pure-tone, bird-like whistles and squeaks, grunts and screeching sounds. Calls are either discrete (very distinct and easily separated by ear into characteristic types), variable (calls made randomly and in great variety of forms) or aberrant (distorted versions of discrete calls).

Discrete calls serve as contact signals – they may be heard at least five miles away – and are used to maintain group cohesion and co-ordinate movements during travel or foraging. Sung in repetitive series, some are emitted in predictable sequences by individual killer whales. Foraging killer whales emit calls in irregular bursts, with long pauses in between. One caller can elicit a chorus of responses from others and small groups working alone call less often. Travelling killer whales call at a much higher rate, in excess of 50 per minute, but compact travelling groups, diving and surfacing simultaneously, are sometimes completely silent.

Variable calls are almost exclusively used when killer whales are close together or socialising. They become highly vocal, producing a cacophony of calls; the more social they are, the noisier they become. Very few discrete calls are made but whistles are common, especially during dives. Changes in behaviour are always accompanied by a sudden onset of vocal activity involving a wide variety of calls.

Head anatomy is uniquely specialised for sound production and reception.

Young killer whales must learn calls; a rarity among mammals. Vocal learning permits greater flexibility in describing details of social and physical environments, better reflecting changes in both. It also permits the development of a repertoire of calls used as a marker for group identity.

Each resident pod has its own unique repertoire of discrete calls, anywhere from 7 to 17. Some are very distinctive, but others are different in subtle ways. Pods share some calls, sometimes with distinctive versions. These differences make up a local dialect. Pods with dialects which overlap are called 'acoustic clans'. Although they may belong to the same acoustic clan, pods sharing calls may not always travel together.

Killer whales maintain dialects over long periods through strong social and behavioural bonding

The marine environment is ever-changing
and ever-challenging. Sound is the best
orientational tool available to killer
whales and smaller dolphins.

among pod members. Differences probably occur through the vocal idiosyncrasies of individual killer whales and the accumulation of errors in the copying of calls across generations. Pod genealogies are probably more accurately traced through common traits in shared calls rather than by assessing which pods associate together.

Compared to resident killer whales, transients are quiet, making calls only during play and after a kill (perhaps to avoid attracting the attention of residents), or as a technique for hunting marine mammals. They commonly produce calls and echolocation clicks together and have small repertoires of discrete calls, from 4 to 7 types. Transient calls are distinct from any produced by resident killer whales. However, transient pods from California, Southeast Alaska and British Columbia share at least one call type, suggesting their acoustic tradition extends over a coastal range of more than 2,500 km (1,552.5 miles).

Vision has secondary usefulness.

Norwegian resident killer whales calls are different yet again, especially in structure. At least one complex call from Norway matches an Icelandic call. It was made by killer whales which arrived in the Norwegian fjords much later than other pods and remained socially aloof during their stay. Although the extent of geographical isolation between killer whales observed in Iceland and Norway remains unknown, acoustic research may yet prove a connection.

Even captive killer whales emit the common calls given by their natal pod, unchanged despite long years of separation. They also learn the dialects of their tank companions, who may have come from halfway around the world.

*Groups co-ordinate their activities using
communication calls.*

The many faces of a killer whale's habitat.

*Pods have their own dialects which
help them recognise each other. Killer whales
from different parts of the world can learn
each other's calls.*

Captivity and Conservation

Merlin lay at the surface, barely submerging after each breath, his 6 foot dorsal fin quivering in the golden peach glow of sunset. The rest of J pod floated nearby, all resting before the big push northwards. Fluffy, rose-tinted clouds floated in a piercing blue sky and the glassy waters reflected dark fins and the sky's fire. It seemed the perfect picture of family harmony, a cliché in a nature film. Only a few years previously, J pod had been one of the most heavily harvested groups for live capture operations. We wondered if its missing members were faring well in captivity, and thought of the great difference between these wild creatures and those performing on command in aquariums, knowing the one can never truly depict the other. And we had to ask ourselves if our work was helping this community of killer whales, or was an intrusion causing unknown detriment.

Personal Diary, October

As ambassadors for their species, it cannot be denied that captive killer whales have educated and entertained millions of people annually, helping to change the public's perception of killer whales. People are now so well-informed that the validity of keeping killer whales in aquariums has become a public issue.

The first killer whale ever to be captured was in California. In 1961, a small female floundered into Newport Harbour. She was corralled with small boats and nets and transported to Marineland of the Pacific, in south Los Angeles. She swam around her tank at high speed, eventually rammed into the sides and died the same day. The autopsy revealed she was 25, with very worn teeth, and suffering from acute gastro-enteritis and pneumonia. Although a failure, the capture showed it was possible to seize and handle killer whales.

Marineland collectors went to Puget Sound the following year. A female was lassoed, but the line got caught in the propeller. She began vocalising loudly and a male joined her in attacking the boat; slapping it with their tail flukes. Panicked, the collectors shot at them, eventually killing the female. Needless to say, this temporarily discouraged further attempts.

The next capture was undertaken in the name of art, in 1964. The Vancouver Aquarium intended to kill a killer whale so that a commissioned artist could have accurate measurements to create a realistic sculpture for display. After two months, a small killer whale was harpooned, but not killed. Instead, it was towed 30 km (18.6 miles) to Vancouver and placed in a newly-constructed floating pen. Incorrectly named 'Moby Doll', the young male refused to eat for two months. Eventually he began, eating 90 kg (198 lbs) of fish per day. Although he died a month later, Moby Doll proved killer whales could be tamed.

Namu was the next captive, in 1965. Accidentally caught in a fishing net in northern British Columbia, he was bought by the owner of the Seattle Aquarium for $8,000 and towed 700 km to Seattle in a floating pen. Namu lived for a year in captivity, and was seen by thousands of visitors being stroked by people and interacting with them. Namu proved killer whales could be loveable and trained to perform. The terrible reputation of killer whales began to fade and captures for aquarium display began in earnest.

The inland waterways of Washington State and British Columbia were the perfect hunting ground. Killer whales were entrapped in the narrow channels and adjacent bays. Entire groups were encircled and a few of the best individuals selected. The ideal captive was a young male, small enough to transport, but guaranteed to grow into an impressive performer. Over the next 11 years an additional 65 killer whales were captured in the region, although some died during the capture operations.

By the end of 1976, when the last capture was permitted in British Columbia and Washington, 17 captive whales from this region were still alive. Public attitudes had changed dramatically.

Killer whales were no longer seen as deadly beasts, but as highly intelligent and loveable symbols of the environmental movement. The public didn't want the whales captured anymore; they wanted them protected. The 'First International Killer Whale Symposium' was held at The Evergreen State College in Olympia, Washington, situated at the southern extent of Puget Sound.

Ironically, capture boats encircled a group of six whales just a few miles from Olympia. Hundreds of people converged on the scene and one of the state governor's assistants witnessed the capture from his

Small bays, like this one off San Juan
Island in Washington State, are typical sites
for corralling killer whales during capture
operations.

sailboat. The state legislature had already been discussing the formation of a killer whale sanctuary in Puget Sound. Because public sympathy was with the whales, it soon became a political issue. The state attorney general filed suit against the operators. While the courts were debating the issue, three of the whales escaped. Eventually, a judge ruled that the remaining whales should be released and invalidated permits for captures in Washington waters.

Although this ended captures in Puget Sound, within a few months, American operators began entrapments off the coast of Iceland. Captures in this part of the Atlantic are now the jurisdiction of Icelandic operators.

Captive killer whales rate higher than bottlenose dolphins in trainability and reliability. Their highly social nature, natural curiosity, playfulness and fearlessness make it possible for them to adapt well to captivity and training. The oldest animal in captivity is 22 years old. However, the survival rate in captivity is less than in the wild, and the mortality of captive-born calves has been high. Factors range from possible complications at birth and general poor health (even adults are susceptible to infection and disease in artificial confines), to parental inexperience. In the wild, killer whale females may gain training in calf-rearing from older females, or may get experience by practising with younger siblings. Females used in breeding programmes collected before maturation might simply not know how to be mothers.

Behavioural problems also arise, usually in response to undue stress caused by restraint, strained relations between tank-mates, or poor rapport with trainers. Trainers have sustained injuries from ramming or crushing when leaping performers abort a routine. In 1991, a trainer was hauled around a tank and drowned by an aggravated captive. In 1989, a long-standing conflict between a killer whale from the Pacific Ocean and one from Iceland ended in death, when one rammed the other.

Stress also arises from boredom and living in an artificial environment. It is difficult, if not impossible, to design a tank large enough to suit a 4 ton animal that can travel over 80 km (49.7 miles) per day in the wild. The complexity of the ocean environment can never be fully reproduced in a concrete tank, no matter how well designed. Most importantly, the social environment of the extended killer whale family is missing in captivity.

Large males are impressive ambassadors for killer whales.

Release programmes have been considered for captive killer whales, stimulated by increasingly obsolete facilities and successful efforts to send captive bottlenose dolphins back into the wild. Releases are hotly debated by those who consider no cetaceans should be captive, and others who worry that long-term captives may not be able to survive in the wild. The problems range from killer whales trying to gain acceptance back into the highly structured communities of their origin (assuming they can be identified) or into any social group, to disease transmission either from 'domesticated' whales into a wild group or vice versa. Yet, carefully done, release programmes might meet some degree of success. Although very expensive, they could open new doors to understanding killer whale social structure and lead the way into a new era for using them as ambassadors in captivity.

In the wild, habitat degradation is probably the greatest problem faced by killer whales. Oil spills and other environmental disasters not only poison killer whales unlucky enough to be caught in them, but they also poison the marine environment, affecting the entire food chain. Even seemingly innocuous building activities can have deleterious effects by causing erosion and destroying watersheds important to fresh-water spawning fish, a major food source for some killer whale communities. In fresh and salt water, heavy silting smothers eggs and fish alike, raises temperatures and reduces oxygen levels in the water. The result is depleted fish stocks and increased competition for killer whales with other marine mammals and man.

Fishermen have often clashed with killer whales, some believing they are serious competitors; even today bullets and dynamite are fired at killer whales to protect fisheries. Killer whales have been accused of frightening fish and ruining shoals. They have been considered particularly threatening by Faroese herring and mackerel fishermen, Alaskan blackcod fishermen, and salmon fishermen in British Columbia and Washington State. In 1956, Icelandic fishermen in the Greenland halibut fisheries became so alarmed that the US Navy was requested to rid the coastal waters of killer whales.

Having learned to exploit fishing boats, killer whales wait nearby, snatching fish falling out of nets or eating netted fish and tearing nets, costing up to 25,000 dollars apiece, in the process. They also take fish off hooked lines, removing the body and leaving the head containing the hook. Yet the exploitation is

The rubbing rocks at Robson Bight are part of an ecological reserve for Canadian killer whales.

mutual: salmon boats set nets in the path of foraging killer whales, and mackerel boats track them on ships' sonars to locate schooling fish.

Killer whales, especially those populations which feed on marine mammals, are already registering high levels of industrial toxins. The world's arsenal of toxic chemicals eventually ends up in the marine environment, deposited directly from ships, nearshore drainage, and rivers, where they not only directly affect organisms, but are taken up by plants and into the food chain. Permanently stored in fatty tissues, toxins become more and more concentrated as predator eats prey. Top predators end up with the jackpot. A particularly cruel pattern of toxin concentration also occurs between mother and calf. Unborn calves absorb toxins through the bloodstream and young calves feed on mothers' polluted, yet rich, fatty milk – the equivalent of double cream. Even before they start hunting on their own, they may have high toxin concentrations.

Habitats also need protection.

Killer whales have never been especially prized for their meat or oil, yet they are hunted in various parts of the world. Over 2,000 killer whales were taken by Norway between 1938 and 1981. Small, coastal operations off Japan have taken up to 150 killer whales annually since the 1950s. Russian whalers have always caught a few in Antarctica, catching a record number of 916 in 1980.

The impact of removing animals from a population is unknown. However, there are individual whales in Norway which form only seasonal alliances, appearing with different pods each year. Although whalers tried to catch full groups, these individuals may be those few which escaped and are now trying to immigrate into some distantly-related pods. In the Pacific Northwest, the differences between the northern and southern resident communities in age and sex structure and reproductive rates are the result of early capture operations which removed prime individuals from the population. Yet, until captive breeding programs become more successful, captures will probably continue. No one can tell whether killer whales would be driven from their home territories or their social fabric destroyed if removals continue. And we have yet to assess other, seemingly benign human activities which impact wild killer whales. The increasingly popular pastime of boat-based whale-watching activities may have long-term effects equally detrimental: increased stress from constant boat traffic, noise disturbance, and habitat degradation, to name just a few. Research activities also lie in this balance between intrusion and consideration.

The combination of long lives, slow maturation rates, variable birth rates and very slow population growth implies extremely slow recovery of any affected stock, taking several generations. Yet, because killer whales are not recognised as being endangered, and are still not considered particularly important natural resources in countries other than Canada and the United States, they receive no special protective status or legislation.

The US Marine Mammal Protection Act of 1972 has numerous provisions for protecting marine mammals, ranging from banning all import/export of marine mammal products, to the protection of habitat and prosecution for harassment. Researchers, film-makers and whale-watching activities are required to obtain a permit from the US Marine Mammal Commission to conduct activities closer than 100 m (109.4 yds); violation of this order leads to prosecution and a fine of up to $10,000. The government of the United States has also designated various marine habitats as protected marine sanctuaries, many of which are important to killer whales. Similarly, Canada created the Robson Bight–Michael Bigg Ecological Reserve on Vancouver Island, to protect the all-important rubbing rocks of the northern resident killer whale community. This area had been under threat by logging operations during the 1970s and 1980s. Pressure from scientists, environmental groups and the public caused the government of British Columbia to take action.

This sort of public action, from the people who know and care about killer whales, and the delicate balance of their marine habitat, is the best protection for killer whales. Hopefully, as we continue to sort the myths from the realities about killer whales, we will only gain a greater, richer appreciation for them as one of Nature's most powerful representatives. Without killer whales, some of the earth's magic would be lost.

Enjoying Killer Whales

Killer whales, with their tall dorsal fins and striking markings, often in large, active groups, are some of the most impressive cetaceans to see in the wild. There is a certain skill to being in the right place at the right time. In the UK, the Hebrides, Orkney and Shetland Islands, off the coast of Scotland, are frequented by small groups of killer whales during summer and fall. The inland marine waters of Washington State and British Columbia are the best location to find killer whales from shore or boat, from July to September. San Juan Island, in northern Washington and in the core area for southern resident killer whales, boasts America's only official whale-watching park where killer whales pass just off the rocks. The Robson Bight–Michael Bigg Ecological Reserve on Vancouver Island, BC and in the core area for northern resident killer whales, is the Canadian equivalent.

Boat-based whale-watching should be undertaken through sanctioned excursions or other natural history expeditions. Be sure to contact local environmental organisations or research groups to find out which whale-watching trips are best. Most will have skilled naturalists who enhance the experience of seeing cetaceans and crews on experienced expeditions are conscientious towards cetaceans' well-being.

It is important to remember that we are unsolicited visitors to a killer whale's habitat and we must treat them, and all cetaceans, with respect. After all, they are wild creatures, with their own criteria for proper social etiquette; ask yourself if you would walk freely while on an African safari, in the middle of the savannahs.

The recommended code of conduct for encountering cetaceans follows common sense. Never block or divert their passage, approach no closer than 100 m (109.4 yds) and never from directly in front. Always remain off to the side or behind the group and keep to the speed of the group without sudden accelerations. Never swim near or attempt to touch cetaceans. Should one solicit your attention, remember that their overtures may appear similar to ours but can have different meaning and results: one woman was recently bitten when attempting contact with curious and friendly pilot whales.

Violation of any of these guidelines constitutes harassment and can cause discomfort and even distress to any cetacean. It also turns whale-watching into an artificial experience, not much different from seeing them on television or in an aquarium.

Killer Whale Facts

Common name	Killer Whale or Orca	
Scientific name	*Orcinus orca*	
Body Meaurements	Female	Male
Maximum Adult Length	8.5 m (9.30 yds)	9.7 m (10.61 yds)
Average Adult Length	5.8 m (6.34 yds)	6.7 m (7.33 yds)
Average Adult Weight	2750 kg (6,064 lbs)	4000 kg (8,820 lbs)
Dorsal Fin Height	0.9 m (.98 yd)	1.8 m (1.96 yds)
Length at birth	2.1 m (2.3 yds)	2.1 m (2.3 yds)
Gestation (months)	15	
Age at maturity (years)	15	21
Longevity (years)	80	50–60

Longevity – The maximum longevity for female killer whales is around 80 years old. Maximum longevity for males is shorter, probably around 50 or 60 years.

Distribution – Killer whales are distributed throughout all oceans and may be seen at all latitudes. However, the majority of concentrations are in the cooler, continental shelf waters of mid to high-latitudes.

Recommended Reading

The most comprehensive reports on the long-term studies of killer whales in Washington and British Columbia have been published in a Report of the International Whaling Commission, Special Issue No. 12, *Individual Recognition of Cetaceans* 1980. Earlier studies were collected in the volume *The Behavioral Biology of Killer Whales*, edited by Barbara Kirkevold & Joan Lockard, A. R. Liss, 1986.

The best popular account of killer whales is Erich Hoyt's *Orca: The Whales Called Killer*, Camden House, Ontario, Canada, 1984. Guides to areas for seeing killer whales are *The Whale Watcher's Handbook* by Erich Hoyt, Doubleday & Co., Inc., Garden City, N.Y. 1984, and *Where the Whales Are* by Patricia Corgan, The Globe Pequot Press, Chester, CT. 1991.

Biographical Notes

Sara L Heimlich-Boran has been studying cetaceans since the mid-1970s. She holds a Masters in Marine Science from Moss Landing Marine Laboratories, San Jose State University, USA. She is currently writing popular and scientific works and is employed by the Sea Mammal Research Unit, Cambridge, England. She lives in Cambridge, England with her husband and 10 year old daughter.

James R Heimlich-Boran has been studying cetaceans since the mid-1970s. He holds a Ph.D from the University of Cambridge, England. He is currently Programme Manager of the Sea Watch Foundation in Oxford, England, organising a public sighting system on the distribution and abundance of whales and dolphins in the British Isles. He lives in Cambridge, England with his wife and daughter.